THE HISTORY OF DREAM CATCHER

Dream Catcher Story

DREAM CATCHER

Designs

Copyright © 26/1/2023 DREAM CATCHER Designs All rights reserved

The characters and events portrayed in this book are fictitious. Any similarity to real persons, living or dead, is coincidental and not intended by the author.

No part of this book may be reproduced, or stored in a retrieval system, or transmitted in any form or by any means, electronic, mechanical, photocopying, recording, or otherwise, without express written permission of the publisher.

ISBN-13: 9798375062341
ISBN-10: 1477123456

Cover design by: Art Painter
Library of Congress Control Number: 2018675309
Printed in the United States of America

DEDICATION

THIS BOOK IS DEDICATED TO THE ALL WHO INTERESTED OF THE DREAM CATCHER HISTORY.

TABLE OF CONTENT

INTRODUCTION

HISTORY OF DREAM CATCHER

USES OF DREAM CATCHER

MORE USES

LIMITATION OF DREAM CATCHER

A Few Examples Of How Dream Catchers Are Used In Different Cultures And Traditions

SUMMARY OF DREAM CATCHER

REFERENCES

INTRODUCTION

A dream catcher is a craft object traditionally made by Native Americans. It is a hoop, often made of willow, that is woven with a web of string or cord, and decorated with feathers and beads. The dream catcher is said to filter out bad dreams, allowing only good dreams to pass through to the sleeper. The good dreams are said to slide down the feathers to the sleeper, while the bad dreams are trapped in the webbing and destroyed by the morning light.

Dream catchers are typically hung above a person's bed and are believed to protect the sleeper from nightmares. They are often given as gifts to children or loved ones, to protect them while they sleep.

The Ojibwe people, an indigenous people of North America, have a longstanding tradition of making and using dream catchers. The legend behind the dreamcatcher says that the spider woman, Asibikaashi, in the Ojibwe culture, would visit the people in their dreams and take away the bad dreams and give good dreams. The dreamcatcher is said to have originated with the Ojibwe people, but it has since been adopted by other Native American tribes and cultures.

Dreamcatchers are made in different sizes, but most commonly are circular, with a diameter of around 6-8 inches. The hoop is usually made of willow, which is bent and woven together to form a circular shape. The webbing is then woven through the hoop, and the dreamcatcher is decorated with feathers and beads. The feathers are said to represent the breath of life and the beads are said to represent the tears of joy. The dreamcatcher is considered a sacred object that should be treated with respect.

Dreamcatcher has become a popular decorative item and many people hang it in their homes to bring good luck, peace and harmony. It has also been used as a symbol of cultural appropriation. Many people have started to use it without understanding its significance and meaning in the Native American culture.

HISTORY OF DREAM CATCHER

The history of the dream catcher can be traced back to the Ojibwe people, an indigenous nation of North America. According to Ojibwe oral tradition, the dream catcher was created by the Spider Woman, known as Asibikaashi, who was responsible for taking care of the children and the people of the tribe. She used to visit the people in their dreams and take away the bad dreams, and give good dreams. She taught the Ojibwe people how to make dream catchers so that they could protect themselves from bad dreams and nightmares.

The dream catcher was originally made by the Ojibwe people using willow hoops and sinew or cord. The hoop was woven with a web of string, and decorated with feathers and beads. The dream catcher was hung above a person's bed, and it was believed to filter out bad dreams, allowing only good dreams to pass through to the sleeper. The good dreams were said to slide down the feathers to the sleeper, while the bad dreams were trapped in the webbing and destroyed by the morning light.

The dream catcher tradition was passed down through generations of Ojibwe families, and it eventually spread to other Native American tribes and cultures. The dream catcher became a symbol of unity and continuity among the tribes. In the 20th century, the dream catcher began to be popularized outside of the Native American communities, and it has since become a popular decorative item.

It is worth mentioning that today the dreamcatcher is considered by some as a symbol of cultural appropriation, as many non-Native people use dreamcatchers without understanding the significance and meaning of the object in the Native American culture.

Dream catchers have become a popular decorative item in recent years, and many people hang them in their homes to bring good luck, peace, and harmony. However, it is important to note that the dream catcher is a sacred object that has deep cultural significance for the Ojibwe people and other Native American tribes. The tradition of making and using dream catchers is an important part of the Ojibwe culture, and it should be respected and understood in that context.

The dream catcher is not just a decorative item, but it has a spiritual meaning for the Ojibwe people. It is considered a powerful tool for protection and healing. The dream catcher is believed to filter out bad dreams and negative energy, allowing only good dreams and positive energy to reach the sleeper. It is also believed to have the power to bring good luck and prosperity to the household.

It is important to note that the dream catcher is not a universal symbol, it is a specific symbol of the Ojibwe people, and other Native American tribes. The dreamcatcher has been used without understanding its significance and meaning by some non-Native people, which could be considered as cultural appropriation, and disrespectful to the Ojibwe people and other native tribes' culture.

In conclusion, the dreamcatcher is a unique and important part of the Ojibwe culture. It is a sacred object that has deep spiritual significance and it should be respected, understood and appreciated in that context. It is important to be mindful of the cultural context when using or displaying a dreamcatcher and to educate oneself about the history, significance and meaning of the object.

The dream catcher has become a popular decorative item in recent years, but it's important to remember that it is a sacred object with deep cultural significance for the Ojibwe people and other Native American tribes. The dream catcher is not just a decorative item, but it has a spiritual meaning and it is considered a powerful tool for protection and healing.

There are some places where you can find authentic dream catchers, made by Native American artisans, and it is important to buy these authentic dream catchers rather than the mass-produced versions that are often sold in souvenir shops, as it helps to support the Native American communities and preserve their traditional practices.

Also, it's important to educate yourself about the history, significance, and meaning of the dreamcatcher, not only to avoid cultural appropriation but also to truly appreciate and understand the object.

Additionally, when displaying a dreamcatcher, it is important to treat it with respect, and to hang it in a place where it will not be damaged or disturbed. It is also important to remember that the dreamcatcher is not just a decorative object, but it has a spiritual significance and should be respected as such.

In general, it's important to be mindful of the cultural context when using or displaying a dreamcatcher and to educate oneself about the history, significance, and meaning of the object. This will help to show respect for the Ojibwe people and other Native American tribes, and to appreciate the dreamcatcher for what it truly is - a sacred and meaningful object with deep cultural roots.

USES OF DREAM CATCHER

Dream catchers are traditionally used by the Ojibwe people and other Native American tribes for a few different purposes:

Protection: Dream catchers are believed to filter out bad dreams and negative energy, allowing only good dreams and positive energy to reach the sleeper. This is why they are often hung above a person's bed.

Healing: The dream catcher is believed to have the power to bring good luck, peace and harmony to the household, and also to promote healing. Some people may hang a dream catcher in a room where someone is recovering from an illness, to help them heal faster.

Cultural Significance: The tradition of making and using dream catchers is an important part of the Ojibwe culture and other Native American tribes, and it is considered a symbol of unity and continuity among the tribes.

Decorative: Dream catchers have become popular decorative items and many people hang them in their homes to bring good luck and positive energy.

It's worth noting that in some cultures and tradition, dreamcatchers are not only used for protection during the night but also as a spiritual tool for protection and guidance during the day. The dreamcatcher's web is a symbol of the spider web, and the spider is a powerful symbol of creation, and its web a symbol of the connection between all living things.

MORE USES

In some cultures and traditions, dreamcatchers are not only used for protection during the night, but they are also considered to have spiritual significance and power during the day. The dreamcatcher's web is a symbol of the spider web, and the spider is a powerful symbol of creation and is associated with many spiritual meanings, such as:

Connection: The spider web is often seen as a symbol of the connection between all living things, and the dreamcatcher is believed to represent this connection by filtering out bad dreams and negative energy, allowing only good dreams and positive energy to reach the sleeper.

Creativity: The spider is often associated with creativity and the ability to weave one's own destiny. The dreamcatcher, with its intricate web and decorations, is seen as a symbol of the ability to create one's own reality.

Intuition: The spider is often associated with intuition and the ability to see beyond the physical world. The dreamcatcher is believed to help the sleeper access their own intuition and inner wisdom through dreams.

Guardianship: The spider is also seen as a powerful guardian, and the dreamcatcher is believed to act as a guardian while you sleep, protecting you from bad dreams and negative energy.

Symbol of Cultural heritage: The tradition of making and using dream catchers is an important part of the Ojibwe culture and other Native American tribes, and it is considered a symbol of unity and continuity among the tribes.

It is important to note that the meanings and uses of the dreamcatcher can vary depending on the culture and tradition. It's important to understand the cultural context and significance of the dreamcatcher before using it or displaying it in your home.

LIMITATION OF DREAM CATCHER

Dream catchers are a traditional craft object with deep cultural significance for the Ojibwe people and other Native American tribes, but it is important to note that it is not a universally effective tool for protection or healing. It is based on the traditional belief of the Ojibwe people and other Native American tribes, and it may not have the same effect on every individual.

It only works when you believe in its power: The dreamcatcher is believed to work through the power of belief, so if you do not believe in its power, it may not work for you.

It can't prevent all bad dreams: While the dreamcatcher is believed to filter out bad dreams, it cannot prevent all bad dreams or nightmares. Some bad dreams may still get through, despite the presence of a dreamcatcher.

It can't cure illnesses: While the dreamcatcher is believed to have the power to promote healing, it cannot cure illnesses or diseases. It is important to seek medical treatment and not rely solely on the dreamcatcher for healing.

It's not a substitute for professional help: If you are experiencing severe nightmares, sleep disorders, or other sleep-related problems, it is important to seek professional help. The dreamcatcher should not be used as a substitute for professional treatment.

It's not a solution for all problems: The dreamcatcher is a traditional object with deep cultural significance, but it is not a solution for all problems. It should be used in conjunction with other methods of protection and healing, and should not be relied upon as the sole method of protection or healing.

It's important to understand the cultural and traditional context of the dreamcatcher and to not overgeneralize or exaggerate its abilities. It is a powerful symbol with deep spiritual and cultural significance, but it is not a universal solution for all problems. It should be respected and appreciated for what it truly is.

A few examples of how dream catchers are used in different cultures and traditions:

The Ojibwe people, an indigenous nation of North America, have a longstanding tradition of making and using dream catchers. The legend behind the dreamcatcher says that the spider woman, Asibikaashi, in the Ojibwe culture, would visit the people in their dreams and take away the bad dreams and give good dreams.

The Lakota Sioux people of North America also have a tradition of making and using dream catchers. The dreamcatcher is used to filter out bad dreams and negative energy and to promote good dreams and positive energy.

The Navajo people of North America also use dream catchers as a protective symbol. They believe that the dreamcatcher filters out bad dreams and negative energy, and allow only good dreams and positive energy to reach the sleeper.

The Cree people of North America also have a tradition of making and using dream catchers. They believe that the dreamcatcher has the power to bring good luck and prosperity to the household, and to promote healing.

Some people today use dreamcatchers as a decorative item and hang it in their homes to bring good luck, peace, and harmony, they may not have any specific cultural or traditional context.

It's worth noting that the meaning and uses of the dreamcatcher can vary depending on the culture and tradition, and it is important to understand the cultural context and significance of the dreamcatcher before using it or displaying it in your home.

SUMMARY OF
DREAM CATCHER

A dream catcher is a craft object traditionally made by Native Americans, specifically by the Ojibwe people. It is a hoop, often made of willow, that is woven with a web of string or cord, and decorated with feathers and beads. The dream catcher is said to filter out bad dreams, allowing only good dreams to pass through to the sleeper. The good dreams are said to slide down the feathers to the sleeper, while the bad dreams are trapped in the webbing and destroyed by the morning light. Dream catchers are typically hung above a person's bed and are believed to protect the sleeper from nightmares. They are often given as gifts to children or loved ones, to protect them while they sleep. The dream catcher is considered a sacred object that should be treated with respect. It's important to be mindful of the cultural context when using or displaying a dreamcatcher and to educate oneself about the history, significance, and meaning of the object.

REFERENCES:

UPWORK.

FIVERR.

www.ingramcontent.com/pod-product-compliance
Lightning Source LLC
Chambersburg PA
CBHW050325220526

45465CB00005B/2141